S0-AXM-555

Still Loving Your Long-Distance Relationship

Stephen Blake
&
Kimberli Bryan

Anton
Anton Publishing Inc. * Canada

Published by
Anton Publishing Inc.
305 Madison Ave.
Suite 1166
New York, New York 10165

Cover art by: Sterling Shanski.

Printed in Canada.

ISBN 0-9680971-3-8

With love, we dedicate this book to all of those in long-distance relationships throughout the world, and to the thousands of people who sent us stories and letters for possible inclusion in *Still Loving Your Long-Distance Relationship.*

While we couldn't use everything you sent in, we were touched by your stories and your willingness to share your hearts with us.

Your friends,

Stephen Blake & Kimberli Bryan

Introduction

Do long-distance relationships work? Without a doubt, this has been the question I've been most commonly asked since I published *Loving Your Long-Distance Relationship* over a year ago. Whether the question is posed by a skeptic trying to prove that long-distance relationships do not work, or by a young couple who find themselves separated by circumstance, people seem intensely interested in whether any LDR has a hope of lasting in today's society. After all, doesn't absence automatically mean the end of a relationship? Doesn't everyone grow apart eventually? What about the loneliness? Won't someone eventually cheat or lose interest in the other? It's inevitable! Or is it?

I admit, when I first started writing my book, I too was skeptical about long-distance relationships. At the time, I had already been through two that ended up in partings. I had also witnessed numerous friends who tried and failed in similar circumstances. Everything seemed fine until distance entered into the relationship. It wasn't until I published *Loving* and started getting letters from people across the world in the same situation, that I realized my skepticism was ill-founded, and that true love always seems to find a way.

Since the release of *Loving*, I have received literally thousands of letters and e-mail from people who have conquered distance in their relationship and now live happily ever after. Whereas I expected accounts of how individuals had experienced a break-up of their relationship, I received stories of couples whose physical separation only served to strengthen their resolve and love for one another. Letter after letter was a testament to love and to the human spirit, reaffirming that LDRs can and do work. Although all agreed that their situation was difficult at times, true love seemed to triumph in the end. Relationships built on solid foundations such as trust, love, and commitment could not, and would not, be shaken by mere absence.

The following pages are a collection of some of my favourite stories that I have received throughout the last two years from my readers and also from those just wanting to share their feelings about their relationship. They have been my inspiration and connection to people who refused to let distance devalue their relationship. They have made writing *Loving Your Long-Distance Relationship* one of the most special and rewarding things that I have ever done in my life.

Whether you are entering into a long-distance relationship, in one presently, or supporting someone who is facing being apart from a loved one, I hope you find these letters as inspiring as I have. I hope they make you feel that there are others like you across the world who have faced the same challenge and won. I hope they instill in you the belief that love transcends geography. Finally, I hope these stories show that it is relationships that make life special, and that ones built on love & understanding are always worth preserving, regardless of the miles that may separate two people.

- Stephen Blake

Letters from the Heart

Miss your partner, sleep in his shirt, listen to 'your' song, tell him how much you love and miss him, and in the end, you'll both be closer and will appreciate each other more fully and completely than otherwise possible.

I just read Loving Your Long-Distance Relationship after my mom sent it to me in a care package at university. There's one of your key support systems: family and friends! Sometimes I think my friends and family want our relationship to work as much as he and I do. I'm going to university on the east coast of Canada, and my boyfriend, Serge, is thousands of kilometres away in Espanola, Ontario. I could identify with most of the points in your book and I just wanted to add a few ideas for anyone else going through this.

Since you and your partner are apart, do you find yourself identifying with mushy, sad, and sappy love songs? Do you find yourself daydreaming about your boyfriend singing them to you, or you to him? If so, you've got it bad! You are in love and missing that person! But those empty, sad, and helplessly romantic feelings you're having while your partner is so far away are exactly what will get you through this.

I loved my boyfriend before I left for university, but it wasn't until we were apart that we both realized that we truly needed each other. Now we know that we don't want anyone else... and that's what real love is all about. In my boyfriend's eyes, I can see my present and my future. I can see that apartment we're going to live in next year... together. I can see the children we're going to have and I can see us growing old with each other. And when we're apart, I can hear all of this in his voice and in the way he tells me he loves me.

If you're starting a long-distance relationship, or you're in one, missing him is only the result of loving him. When I miss Serge, I call him to hear his voice, or I put on his sweater just to be close to his smell. I wear his necklace and every time the charms click together, I think of him. Sure it hurts, but I wouldn't trade missing him for not missing him. I know missing him reflects our love and I also know I'll see him again, sometime.

Long-distance couples gain a real appreciation for each other that regular couples may never have. I appreciate every sweet thing Serge does for me and I now know I'll never take him for granted. I know how lonely it is and how hard it is to be apart from him, so never will I take for granted the gift I have found in him.

Long-distance relationships are hard, but they definitely can work! So by all means, miss your partner, sleep in his shirt, listen to 'your' song, tell him how much you love and miss him. In the end, you'll both be closer and will appreciate each other more fully and completely than otherwise possible.

I've found my other half and I'm content in waiting for next year when all of the plans we make in our late night phone calls will really come to be.

You give excellent advice for dealing with bumps in the road. I just want people to appreciate how lucky they are to be in love and be loved! And to let them know that the time when they'll finally be with their loved one will come sooner, rather than later.

- Faith

The time we spend together is a million times better than the couples who see each other every day and take it for granted.

♡♡♡

I got a job at the library in my hometown about thirteen months ago. A few days later, I was introduced to my soon-to-be girlfriend, Galina. We started going out and we've had some hard times, but staying together has made me as happy as I could possibly be.

The problem was that before I met her, I had applied to the colleges I liked, all of which happened to be outside of New York State. I chose the University of Maryland at College Park and I like it, but it's so sad without her here. I talk to her every day for as long as I possibly can. I send her letters every so often and she does the same for me. It's hard not having her around every day and I miss her a lot. During parent weekend, she came down here with my family and I got to be with her the whole time, parent-free. I missed her soooooo much and I realized that staying together was the best choice we ever made, because although we didn't go out much during those two days, I can happily say that I had the best time of my entire life. I missed her and she missed me and because we care for each other that much, the time we spend together is a million times better than the couples who see each other every day and take it for granted.

The point is that couples need to realize who they have in front of them, and if they don't appreciate it, then all the things that they love about their significant other could disappear without warning. We love each other more than any couple I've ever heard of. I know that we are both young, but that doesn't stop me from shooting high. I want to marry my girlfriend and I know *that* in my heart. That is the main reason our relationship has been so successful thus far. We love each other with all of our hearts and we put all of our hearts into our relationship.

People tell me they wouldn't do what I'm doing because they can't make a commitment like that. Well, my girlfriend means just about everything to me, and I want nothing more than to be with her for the rest of my life. Some people want to be rich or famous or to be president. I guess I'm a simple man because if I have Galina, then I'll be just fine.

- Seth

True love will stand the test of time and distance.

Eric and I have been dating for six years and we have been best friends for seven. Having a long-distance relationship is nothing like what I was expecting. This is the eighth week of our LDR. Before he left, I didn't think 500 miles was too far apart. I didn't think I would actually cry when he is not around. I thought it would be good for us to be apart to test our relationship, plus I would have my own time to do my own things.

During the first two weeks when we were apart, I decided anything more than 30 miles was far away. I cried daily or even hourly when I was alone. It was a test all right... a test to see how much work I could accomplish without having him on my mind. I had a hard time focusing on just my regular job, not to mention the extra things I'd planned on doing!

Now that eight weeks have passed, I'm starting to get used to it. Five hundred miles has become a distance worth driving. No more tears, only smiling faces when thoughts of him cross my mind. I got the results from the test: I love him more than I thought and our relationship is stronger than I imagined. Work is back to normal and I am following my original plans and doing things that are long overdue.

I miss him very much but I am even happier to know, with no doubts in my mind, that he is definitely that special someone. All I need now is some patience to enrich what I already have.

- Judy

The hardest part of this is knowing that the reason this may not work out isn't because of us, but because of distance.

I was surfing the net late one evening, missing the girlfriend from my long-distance relationship, when I typed in the words, "long-distance love". That's when the website for your book came up.

I met my girlfriend while she worked one summer with me at a camp in Maine. She is from Poland and I am from Maine. We were together for only a month or so and we formed a great friendship that turned into a great relationship. We spent as much time together as we could because we both knew she had to return to Poland for another year at her university. What is even more difficult is that she needs to stay in Poland to finish her education and I am just starting a new leg of my career as a teacher, so we both have commitments for the near future.

We spent some time together after our work was completed and went on vacation. When it was time for us to part, neither of us wanted it to happen. We sat at the train station and held each other for what seemed to be hours. This is the hardest thing I've ever had to cope with. Sylvia called me several times from different places she visited. Each time we felt this relationship become stronger and stronger. The final time she called, just before flying home, we were both crying and didn't want this to end. It was very hard for me to hang up the phone. I was an emotional wreck for weeks after she left the country.

We discussed our relationship before we parted and knew this was going to be difficult. Sylvia said that we didn't know what would happen in our futures and I agreed.

I just flew to Poland to be with her for Christmas and New Year's. Our love for each other hasn't faded at all. In fact, it has become even stronger. We shared a wonderful week together. Instead of watching her fly home, she was watching me. She made me promise not to cry so that she wouldn't. I tried, but as I was leaving for the gate, I turned to throw her a kiss and saw her wiping tears from her eyes. I couldn't help but start crying myself. For the entire ten hour flight back to Boston, I was crying. Just as I read in your introduction, at the mere thought of her I could feel her warmth, hear her voice, and taste her kisses.

I call to keep in touch and write as often as I can and she does the same. We both want this to continue, but the distance between us is very difficult. I sit at home sometimes and think about her and not having her because of this. My family keeps telling me that this won't work and I am going to be hurt someday. I try to tell them that what is important right now is that we're happy and we will deal with whatever happens when it happens.

The hardest part of this is knowing that the reason this may not work out isn't because of us, but because of distance.

- Andrew

We are so in love and we know that no matter what distance there is between us, our hearts and thoughts will always be together

Jeff and I met when he was in his last year of business school at the University of Michigan, at a local student hangout in Ann Arbor. He approached me... and changed my life in ways I never thought I would have seen in my lifetime. Small town girl has become traveller girl; so much for my tidy,

predictable, controlled lifestyle. I love him dearly –
and I'm certain he feels the same way or I would
never have put forth this much effort and emotional
roller coaster riding in any relationship.

It started out picture book nice and comfortable
with our first six months together, living within 45
minutes of each other... and I used to complain about
that! Now the five hours between us feels like cruel
torture. After six months of being together on an
almost daily basis, reality set in and Jeff went back
to Chicago after graduation to take his job in a
consulting firm. You see, Jeff and I are both very
practical people, and for many sage reasons, it was
just not feasible for us to be together at that time. I
have three semesters left of grad school, and if I tried
to transfer, I would lose well over half of my credits.
Also, call me an old-fashioned prude, but this smart
girl just isn't going to give up her life here to go be
with her sweetie on a wish and a prayer. Seal it with
a contract, baby, and I'm there! We also discussed
the idea of Jeff working in Detroit, but no can do. He
just isn't at all interested in working in the auto
industry. Some romantic diehards might accuse my
man (and, actually, I have, too) of a lack of gallantry,

but I would never ask him to take a job he would hate, for the sake of love.

So we see each other when we can. So far, it hasn't been too bad. His new job and my education are keeping us busy. The hardest part is knowing that I can't just get in my car and go see him whenever I want. I wish for the simple things in life, like renting a movie on a Wednesday night, not a weekend night, seeing each other come home at the end of our days, etc. The worst thing of all is that it is such a struggle at times not to argue about the silly little things. The phone does not bring you closer together. We can't read each other's body language or gestures, and it becomes really easy to misread intended messages. So we've yelled, hung up the phone, and threatened breaking up on numerous occasions (that one is past tense now, one of our so-called 'rules' not to be broken). Now we mainly just tell each other how much we love each other, miss each other, and look forward to the next time we either rent a car, hop on the train, or go Greyhound in order to feel that 'real' feeling of actually seeing that human being we talk to so often on the phone. We've talked about marriage -- he more than me, I might add -- but for now, we'll continue to make Ma Bell one enormously rich woman.

- Andrea

The reason I put up with this is because I truly am happier with this then I could ever be with anyone else.

I   t all began last January 4th about 10 p.m. on the computer. I was minding my business when Rich sent me an instant message. He said, "Hey, we have the same birthday..." or something to that effect. He was just browsing AOL and noticed that we share a birthday. In fact, we were born in the same year, only about forty-five miles away from each other. I did come first, though... by eight hours. We e-mailed back and forth a little but nothing much came of it.

Sometime after our meeting, I found out that he lived in Ottawa, and soon after that, I discovered that he'd had my brother-in-law in school as a teacher. Wow, what a coincidence! Anyway, a couple of months went by and we lost touch. Then we met again on AOL one night. I found out that he had a girlfriend, and for some reason, that really upset me. For the next couple of months, we talked almost every day in chat rooms. Then a couple of things happened. We fell in love, we met in person with our best friends, and he broke up with his girlfriend.

After he broke up with her, we finally got to go on our first date. It was awesome. We were so excited to see and be with each other that we did not really see a moment of the movie and those two hours flew by. He asked me to marry him, too. That's how fast we fell in love.

We spent the summer commuting from town to town and still chatting on the net for about an hour every night. It was a wonderful summer except for one thing; it had to end. Rich went to Texas to go to school... and I stayed in Illinois.

We talk every night now. It's hard, but I love him so much and trust him so much. Sometimes all I want is to be in his arms. Actually, that is what I want most of the time. The reason I put up with this is because I truly am happier with this then I could ever be with anyone else. I love him. That is all there is to it. I do it because... well, because he is a really big part of me. A part that I cannot live without.

- Katherine

Absence can make the heart grow fonder.

I'm in a long-distance relationship and have been for over three years. Chris and I were together for two months before his family moved away to Ohio. We were both sixteen at the time. We decided that we were going to give this a try and... so far so good. We're twenty now and still together.

We talk everyday and have phone bills from hell, but it's worth it. We agreed that we weren't going to go more than six months without seeing each other, and so far, we haven't. Lately, it's been more like every three months. But we're both in college and totally broke. I work just to pay my phone bill, basically. We struggle just like in every other 'normal' relationship, but we love each other so much that we wouldn't even think of not being together.

People say that we really aren't together, but just because we aren't in the same zip code does not mean we aren't together. I just wanted you to know that I plan on buying your book and probably getting a copy for Chris for Christmas. And I wanted to thank you for letting people know that there is such a thing as a successful long-distance relationship.

- Laura Anne

We know that no matter what distance there is between us, our hearts and thoughts will always be together.

I love your website! I am originally from Miami, but I go to school in Worcester, Massachusetts. I am a junior in college and have been with my boyfriend for three years. He lives in Miami, which is home for me, and he also goes to school there. It is extremely hard, but completely worthwhile!

We try to see each other every three weeks, but sometimes it doesn't work out that way. I try to accumulate vouchers on the airlines so that I can visit him more often. So many people used to tell me that I was wasting my time but, boy, have I proven them wrong! We are so in love and we know that no matter what distance there is between us, our hearts and thoughts will always be together.

We talk every day, sometimes three times a day. I love to let him know when I'm thinking about him, which is almost every minute of the day. Every time the phone rings, I still get excited and hope it is him. The last couple of days before we see each other, we get very antsy and excited. We act like little kids on Christmas morning! I am really very lucky to have Danny in my life. He makes me smile... through a phone! How many people can do that? He also makes me laugh, cry, and realize how much I really love him. Although there are 1,580 miles between us, we always manage to make it through the tough times and enjoy the good times. My education is very important to me and Danny supports me one hundred percent. He really is my number one fan. I don't know if I could have made it without him and his support and his advice.

We have both been stuck in airports because of snowstorms and we have both been the one crying when the other gets on the plane to leave. But in the end, when I think about saying goodbye -- and I hate to -- and pack my suitcase and put everything else in my life on hold for him, I realize it is so worth it, because he is the most important person in my life, and I don't know what I'd do without him. I would never give up what I have. I am the luckiest girl in the world!

- Rebecca

I know in my heart that good things come to those who wait. For this...I'd wait forever.

Hi! My name is Linda, and I met David over the Internet through a free personals ad. He was searching for Miss Right and I was looking for Prince Charming. I was going to be working in Illinois for the summer, only one hour from where he lived and next door to the town where he grew up. We talked for weeks over e-mail and exchanged pictures.

Never in a million years did I think I would find my soul mate over the Internet. I began to fall in love with him. Before I left for Illinois, he came to Indiana to meet me. We had two awesome weekends together before I left. During the two and a half months that I worked in Illinois, I saw him every weekend. I fell deeply in love with him and I knew that this would go beyond a summer fling. We had similar family lives and values, including strong religious beliefs. We could finish each other's sentences. We had a wonderful summer and I wanted it to never end. But finally it did end. Tearfully, one gray Tuesday morning, I kissed him goodbye, got in my car and drove back to Indiana. We both cried. I cried all the way home.

Now, every weekend, we take turns making the three hour trip. We have huge long-distance bills. I cry every time I leave him. He is in his last year of law school and I am a college junior, and time is a precious commodity. We have been together just six months and already we talk and dream together about our future, the time when we can finally stop all the pain that goes with being apart.

I think even though it is tremendously hard, that being apart has helped us. When we are together, we make every second count. We talk to each other continuously and we are very careful not to sidestep issues when we have disagreements. It is too easy for people in long-distance relationships to let things slide because they don't want to waste time fighting. But being honest about things is the key to building a strong relationship. People need to make sure that it is the person they love, and not the intensity or drama that goes with being in a long-distance relationship.

I have found true love with David. I love him for everything that he is, even 200 miles away from me. I know that forever won't be long enough to spend with him. This test seems so unfair at times, but I know in my heart that good things come to those who wait. For this... I'd wait forever.

- *Linda*

♡♡♡

The one thing that there is an abundance of in a long-distance relationship is time. If one hopes to survive a LDR, one must learn to keep busy and focus on things other than your relationship when your partner is away.
- Stephen Blake

♡♡♡

Jim and I met on AOL almost a year ago. I'm in New Hampshire and he's in Hawaii in the Air Force. We both grew up in the Air Force and that was one thing that attracted us to each other. Plus, I was going through a separation and he and I became friends first.

We met in September, in St. Louis. It was great, like we'd known each other forever. I am 45 and he is 33, which sometimes bothers me, like when people comment about him and his 'mom' -- which happened recently.

In December, I went to Hawaii for a week to visit him. We became closer, shared each other's lives for a week. I know it doesn't sound like much, but we laughed and cried together. He leaves Hawaii in May and I hope to join him sometime this summer. It's very hard with him so far away. We do keep in touch on AOL and the phone. He's very disciplined about keeping our phone bills down. I, however, feel like you... when I need to talk, I talk. We are committed to being together; I certainly wouldn't do this if we weren't. Its hard to be alone; I complain about it all the time. He helps me; he's been alone for years and can cope better than I. He is always on the go, keeping busy. I just got home today from Hawaii... and the pain I feel from missing him is unbearable, but I know we can make it through, because we love each other.

- Marsha

Loving someone, even from afar, means never missing out on anything in life.

My boyfriend and I were neighbours and high school sweethearts. We have been together nearly six years. His dream was to play baseball professionally, so for years he played and we spent many summers apart while he was travelling around the world. Sometimes I would hardly see him at all! But I supported his every move. It sure was hard, but nothing has been harder than the last two years while he was away to school on scholarship in Texas. I was left in Canada, 23 hours away, and without him once again... only for way longer this time.

No matter how many times we have said goodbye to each other, it never seems to get easier. Counting weeks, days, even hours until it's time to go, we still stand, hugging in my doorway, weeping. Before every departure, he whispers, "I love you and you have got to believe it." He means to comfort me... and somehow it always does.

Long-distance calls, huge phone bills, a few letters are all we have to connect. Looking back on a year, we figure that he is barely around for 2 months and I feel that we miss out on so much of our lives that should be shared together, like normal couples. However, we love each other with all our hearts, and that makes our relationship grow even stronger and makes every goodbye a little less hard to say. To this day, our friends and relatives cannot believe how strong we are to have overcome such long distances for so long, still faithful and in love since the day we met. When people tell me they don't know how I can do it, I realize that I don't have a clue how I do it, either! But I think that proves love overcomes all.

One day we hope to be married so we never have to be apart again... but looking to our future, I am afraid that we may always be living a long-distance relationship. There have been days when I want to give up and I feel really low, many nights crying in my bedroom while my friends are going out with their mates and having the time of their lives. There are also days when I feel I can no longer trust him... but then I talk to him again and he tells me everything is going to be all right. And it is! We are still together today. We hardly ever argue, we trust each other completely, and I believe that living through a long-distance relationship like ours, separated by such distance, has brought us closer together. Somehow we are connected not only by the phone but by the heart. I believe that true love will overcome any distance.

- Bonnie

The fun thing about growing apart is that when you finally do get together, you should have a great time getting reacquainted!
- Stephen Blake

I fell in love with a woman who never stops moving... literally! Teresa happens to be a dancer. Only two months into our newfound love, she received a phone call that began our long-distance affair. It was a cruise line asking her to dance in their shows for the next seven months. It didn't hit me that she was really leaving until her plane began roaring down the runway. At that moment, my heart hit the floor.

The first four months apart were a real struggle. Men wooed her on the ship. I had offers of my own.

We both were guilty of forgetting the love we have for each other. When the fifth month came around, we began to talk more openly, and our talks brought us closer every week. I felt I knew her better than when she was home with me. But even with our relationship turning around, my heart still ached to see her.

I booked a trip to Alaska on the MS Veendam. When we first saw each other, I almost didn't know what to say. I thought to myself, "She is more beautiful then I remember!" Our eyes locked and I knew everything was meant to be. The trip was amazing! We hiked to the top of Mt. Roberts in Juneau. We saw wild grouse and even a bear. Teresa made snow angels at the top. Our spirits soared and we felt as 'one'.

That night, back on the ship, we made love for the first time. It was beautiful and romantic. Our reunion in Alaska, as I know now, was only the beginning of a beautiful, almost fairytale love.

- *Stephen*

♡♡♡

A boyfriend doesn't have to be physically there, to be there for you... never settle for less than perfect happiness.

♡♡♡

I, for one, have never been in favour of long-distance relationships. In fact, I almost found them ridiculous! I mean, how could two people carry on with distance being such a physical barrier?

All that changed for me when I met Josh. I had just become a registered user on a popular chat site, not looking for love, but more for an escape. I felt like I was in a rut. I hadn't even graduated from high school yet, and I felt alone in the world. Sure, I had a boyfriend... Dan... but he never understood the "inner" me. One night I came across the handle, Runs With Scissors... and it made me laugh out loud! I told Runs With Scissors that I really liked his/her handle. We started talking with private messages and I found out alot about the person behind that name.

Runs With Scissors was actually Josh, an eighteen-year-old college student with a Journalism major. It was so nice to finally meet a guy with brains! We had similar interests and opinions at that moment on things such as drinking, religion, and school. We parted after about a half hour of conversation, and at that moment in time, I knew he was something special. I had never done anything like this before and my Mother cautioned me. "Be careful, for there are lots of weirdos on the Internet!" she said.

Every day after school, I rushed to the computer and went back to that chat site, looking for Josh. I couldn't give him my e-mail address, because it wasn't working at the time. A mutual friend of ours, Ana, kept telling me that I just missed him! I don't know why, but I couldn't stop thinking about him. I'd never met someone with whom I had so much in common. Unfortunately, it was at least a month before I saw him again. I thought about him nonstop: in class, with my boyfriend, Dan, in my dreams... all the time!

We were reunited at last! I was a little embarrassed to tell him that I was thinking of him after only talking with him once, but I told him that

I'd been looking for him all this time. He said that he was looking for me, too, and we both expressed how nice it was to see each other again. Then he said the words that I will never forget... I got a private message that said, "Michelle, I think I love you." I nearly melted!

I realized that I loved him too. We must have talked online for hours that night, both of us amazed at our feelings for one another. For months we continued our secret meetings in the chat room. We also started talking on the phone (in secret, of course) after six months of chatting. You see, I didn't think anyone would understand. In fact, I didn't even understand!

Then something terrible happened. I decided that I just couldn't do it. Josh lived near Los Angeles and I live in Vancouver. I didn't think it could ever work. Besides, my boyfriend, Dan, was giving me hell for spending so much time on the Internet. It was too much for me to handle. I didn't like the secrecy and I thought that long-distance relationships never worked. And so I told Josh that he could no longer tell me that he loved me or call me. I said that I would be in contact, and I left with that tearful goodbye. Josh was very good about the whole thing.

He never once yelled at me or judged me. He simply stated that he loved me and would do anything for me.

No matter how hard I tried, I couldn't stay away. So many nights I phoned Josh in tears and gasping for air. He always told me that he'd be there for me, no matter what. I realized at that point that I couldn't live without him. Then came the big test. Josh knew that something was bothering me. I couldn't even function anymore, I was a mess. I had just lost my virginity to Dan and I thought that I might be pregnant. Dan did not treat me well, but I thought that a mediocre boyfriend here was better than a wonderful boyfriend far away. I finally broke through the fear, and between sobs, I told Josh what I had done. I sat there, tears streaming down my cheeks, and he still did not judge me. He said that everything would be okay, and that he still loved me, no matter what. He even said that if I was pregnant he'd support whatever decision I made and would even fly out here to be with me through my pregnancy. I couldn't believe it!

Then I knew that Josh was like no other. He was my soul mate and I was truly in love with him. He stayed on the phone with me until the early hours of the morning, listening to my fears and my disgust with myself for doing such a thing when I wasn't ready. He encouraged me to tell my mom and said that it would help. That was one of the hardest times of my life. I ended up telling my mother and everything worked out. I wasn't pregnant and I broke up with Dan. I really believe that everything happens for a reason. Josh has been my guardian angel! I knew from that moment on that he and I would be together forever, and that I could face anything. So, I decided to tell those around me about Josh. I told my mother bits and pieces about him, and at first she was wary, but now she accepts him. Some of my friends didn't understand, but I expected that. At least I had it all out in the open.

Josh and I continued our relationship without seeing each other until the summer, which was about six months. When we first saw each other, our hearts connected! The first time I felt him in my arms, it was like I'd died and gone to heaven! I remember our first kiss like it was yesterday. We were in his hotel room, sitting on his bed gazing at each other. He gently ran his hand through my hair, then to my face. Suddenly, his soft lips were pressed against mine and we were finally connected!

Josh and I have been together for over a year now, and he will be here in Canada for another visit in a week. He has been my heart and soul and my guardian angel. He has taught me so much about myself, and how to love myself for who I am. He has never said a harsh word to me, nor has he ever raised his voice. He has always said that I am free to phone him at any time, night or day, if I need to talk to him about anything. We have shared so much laughter and tears together, so much so that without the other, we feel that we are not complete. When Josh asked me to marry him, my heart cried, "YES!!" He is the only man for me.

I have changed a lot of policies that I had before I met him. For one, a boyfriend doesn't have to be physically there, to be there for you... also I will never settle for less than perfect happiness. With Josh, I have found flawless love. Oh, yeah... and distance has definitely made this heart grow fonder!

- Michelle

♡♡♡

The reason we've survived is because we communicate, we trust each other, and we believe in God to help us.

♡♡♡

I have been in a long-distance relationship for over five years now. My boyfriend, Kevin, is a family friend whom I've known all of my life. When I was thirteen, I developed a crush on him. A few years later, we started writing to each other. Two years after that, when I was seventeen, we started dating... if you want to call it that! I was so scared about starting something like this because I didn't know if it would work out. And if it didn't, would there be tension between our families and what else would happen? But I thought that it was worth the risk because I had cared for him for so long. And that began our long-distance relationship.

Over five years later, we're still together, though still in different cities, just like it began! But we have plans to get married soon. The past five years have not been the easiest, but they have been the best part of my life. When we're apart, we long for each other all of the time. I have become the queen of daydreaming! But he is my strength and my rock. He constantly tries to cheer me up when times are tough. The reason we've survived is because we communicate, we trust each other, and we believe in God to help us. Without that, we wouldn't have made it this far. There is no doubt that this situation has allowed us to grow and mature. It has taken a lot of patience, trust, faith, character, and strength to make it through this, but we've fought hard to make it work and it has. Times are lonely when we're apart, but so wonderful when we're together.

A long-distance relationship is something that I would never wish on anyone. It is one of the hardest things to go through. After five years, I am getting used to saying goodbye, but it is never easy. I know what to expect, and I always tell myself that I'll be okay, but the tears still flow and my heart still feels like it's breaking. The longing and the loneliness never subside. But all of the pain and the heartache are worth it, because he's worth it. When I found your website, I read the introduction with tears in my eyes because it reflected what I've felt for so long now. I know that I am not the only one in the world who is in a long-distance relationship, but sometimes it feels like it, because no one I know has ever been in one and they just don't understand. It is comforting to know that there are others out there who feel my pain and understand. But now there is a light at the end of the tunnel. In a few short months, he is going to be moving to my city so that we can be together. After five years we deserve it! Now I can finally be with the one I love most in this world!

- Robyn

Sometimes distance allows people to become close friends without any pressure for physical intimacy.

In January of this year, I was once again, a bachelor. My dating life had been very selective the past two or three years, and I was quite ready to find that special one I knew was out there. I had been playing in a band with some of my friends and we were looking for a change in our sound, a new singer, preferably female. We had friends of friends who introduced us to Jenny, a red-haired beauty with an angelic voice and a fun spirit. She sang a few lines and she was in. We began practising together and as the weeks passed, Jenny and I began to develop a strong friendship. She lived fifty miles and a long-distance phone call away. Needless to say, we spent our paychecks on phone bills and gasoline.

The Internet provided for a bit of help with our communication. It was a nice medium for poems and quick notes, but waiting for the other to respond took forever. Usually we ended up calling each other instead, to save our frustration.

At nineteen, I was living on my own, but Jenny, twenty-two, had moved back into her parents' house after living out of town. We were both in school -- she at the University of Science and Arts of Oklahoma (USAO) in Chickasha, and I at the University of Oklahoma (OU) in Norman.

By April, we were dating. Jenny had never had a boyfriend before -- offers made by others were turned down as she waited and prayed for the right one. I had dated since middle school, but had yet to find the person I knew God had saved for me.

As we dated, our friendship grew even stronger. I began driving close to one hundred miles every Sunday to attend her church. She drove the same distance (from Anadarko, where her parents lived) at least twice a week for practices and dates together.

By September, on our fifth month anniversary, we were engaged. I had just transferred to her school and moved to Chickasha so that I could be closer to her. We are getting married next month, in December, with complete blessings from our parents and friends.

- Michael

♡♡♡

Our relationship's foundation is communication. I think that is why it has lasted this long. We know that the day we can't tell each other the truth or have to keep something from the other person, then we'll know that we have lost our foundation and our relationship.

I know that just by my age you think that I have no clue what I'm talking about, but I have a good feeling that I do. I've always been the type of person who seemed older, maybe by the way I looked or the way I acted. So when I decided to get into a relationship, I was hoping for a relationship that was going to last me a lifetime. When I was only 15, I met this guy named David. I didn't tell him for a long time that I liked him, but after about six months of talking and getting to truly know him, we decided to get together. Being in high school, everyone knows that a relationship is never going to work because everyone in school is going to butt in and try to 'better' your relationship. But that is not what we wanted. For two and a half years, we've been dealing with the fact that some people give us stares, we lose some friends, and we get nasty comments from people, because he is black and I am Mexican. We thought that was going to be the hard part for us.

But then came the fact that we had to go to college and that we would more than likely be apart from each other. We had talked about what would happen but we never really decided on anything, mainly because we didn't want to face that we were probably going to go to school in different states. David decided to go to the University of Michigan, while I decided to stay in California. I never really dealt with him going to live in Michigan until he told me that he had gotten in. I didn't know whether to congratulate him or cry... because he was going to leave me behind. When June came around, and graduation from high school got closer and closer, it all began to sink in. Crying doesn't express the pain. I thought my world was going to end.

I knew that being in a long-distance relationship was going to be hard, but I figured it would be like all the other times we were apart. So when the time to go our separate ways came, I thought I was well-prepared. Now I look back and see how dumb I was for thinking that it was going to be easy. It was the hardest thing for me to handle. To this day, it is still the hardest thing to handle. No more seeing him every day at school, no more holding hands or kissing, or hugs, or long talks, or watching TV, or making love. This is the man I'm going to marry and now I can't even hold his hand.

For a while, I was mad at him because I always thought that he was leaving me behind because he didn't care. I made him feel so guilty for leaving sometimes, and in the end, I only wound up hurting myself more. As time goes on, you think that the distance between you would seem less and less, but it doesn't. The miles between the two of us are always in the back of my mind as I sit there and talk to him on the phone. My mind and heart go through so many things that I can't even explain.

There was once a time that the loneliness got the best of me and I cheated on David. I can't say that what I did was right, because it wasn't, but for that one night that I was finally with someone, it felt worth it. I was finally being loved; I could actually feel the emotions he was giving to me. I could feel someone holding me and kissing me. I didn't feel alone anymore. After it was all over, and the wholeness wore off, I knew that what I had done could never be taken back or corrected. I thought that I was going to lose David forever because I knew that I could not keep something like this from him. The people that I talked to told me not to tell him because if I just forgot about it, it was going to be all right. I knew in my heart that I had to tell him. I had to pay for my mistake and if that meant losing David forever, then that is what I had to do. I decided to tell him over the phone because a letter would just be worse for him. As the words came out of my mouth, I could feel the pain and the tears through the phone. I wanted to die, but I knew I had to hear everything he had to say before he told me it was over, forever.

Amazingly enough, David didn't leave me. He wasn't mad at me... but he was disappointed in me. His disappointment was worse than being mad at me. He forgave me and we started over. We re-evaluated our relationship to see where we had gone wrong. David said that I may have been the one who cheated but that somewhere in the past, we lost our connection with each other that we had to find, to make sure that this never happens again.

David and I have been in this relationship for four years now and it seems to be getting stronger and stronger. We have both changed since we've been together, but for the good of the relationship. David and I have spent hundreds of dollars on phone bills so that we do not lose touch with each other. We may communicate through e-mail, chat online, and write letters, but it is never good enough unless I hear his voice on the other end of the line. Our relationship's foundation is communication. I think that is why it has lasted this long. We know that the day we can't tell each other the truth or have to keep something from the other person, then we'll know we have lost our foundation and have no more relationship. I pray to God each day that it never comes to that.

Being in a long-distance relationship is hard and it takes very patient people to make it work. If the love is truly there, then I know that David and I will get married after we get out of college. Thank you for hearing my story. It felt good to write about how much I love David and how nothing is ever going to take that love and commitment away from us.

- Christina

Long-distance relationships can work if there's love, trust, understanding, and faith.

Although being in a long-distance relationship will seem difficult at times, if you believe in yourself and your relationship, you're 99% of the way there.

- Stephen Blake

♡♡♡

I found your webpage while at work. Tears came from my eyes after I read the introduction. I'm a 24-year-old Japanese woman in the middle of a long-distance relationship with my boyfriend, Marco, living in Texas. We met in the States and fell in big love. I never thought a long-distance relationship would happen to me. We write e-mails everyday and call once in a while and visit each other. It has been only five months since we've been apart. Over the phone he has cried out how lonely he is without me. I cry on the way home from work. I wish we had never met and I could meet someone else here with whom I could be close. But I know how much I'm loved and I love him. I hope we survive this and are together one day.

- Akiko

"Wouldn't it be easier to have a relationship with someone who lives in the same area?" And to this question, I ask them, "Well, would you rather have convenience or true love?"

It all started about five months ago. I met someone in California, just once, and ever since we've kept in contact through the Internet. She turned out to be the most loving, caring, and sweetest person I've ever met. We both have the same interests, dreams, and aspirations. Chatting on the net turned into letters and long-distance phone calls. I'm a nineteen-year-old guy who found love on the net. She is my girlfriend, Jen.

I'm an aspiring graphics artist and I work part time in a bookstore. (That's how I discovered your book; I immediately picked it off the shelf and bought it.) While I was reading it, I felt like I was reading a biography of myself! I related to all the problems, all the situations that you experienced.

I also related to the part about your family. It took me awhile to face the fact that I had an Internet girlfriend. When friends ask, I now answer them with a strong reply, saying, "Yes, I have a long-distance relationship and I love every second of it!" There are some people out there that can't understand why I'm in a situation like this, and they automatically think negative thoughts about it. I always tell people not to knock it if you haven't tried it.

The way I see it, there are five billion people on this planet and maybe, just maybe, there is this higher force that brought Jen and me together... my soul mate. People say, "Why don't you find someone here in Winnipeg?" I tell them, "Well, I'm happy with Jen and I wouldn't trade her for the world. With all the people on this planet, why must I find love in the place that I live?" They always give the same reply, "Wouldn't it be easier to have a relationship with someone who lives in the same area?" And I have this question that always shuts them up, or just makes them think. I ask them, "Well, would you rather have convenience or true love?"

I've talked to Jen almost every day through the Internet, and it seems like a normal relationship. I send her things all the time like romantic designs or drawings, pictures that I've made, sent via e-mail. To this day, our relationship is still going strong and I love her with all my heart. I plan to move to California, sooner or later, and make a career there.

Well, I guess this is it. It's not much of a story, but to me, it's like a fairy tale... where the ending always turns out good.

- Ian

Time to say goodbye is hard, but it makes us very happy that we miss each other so much and that it will just be a matter of time until we decide to be with each other forever.

♡♡♡

I met my boyfriend while we were both on a cruise. It was love at first sight. We spent the most amazing seven days cruising through the Caribbean Islands. My boyfriend, Anthony, is from New York, and I live in Puerto Rico. Since the cruise, we've stayed together and our relationship has grown. We communicate everyday via e-mail and phone. We also write to each other and travel to see each other at least once a month. Every time we are together, time just seems to fly. We make everything perfect and live life to the fullest, enjoying each other's company. Time to say goodbye is hard, but it makes us very happy that we miss each other so much and that it will just be a matter of time until we decide to be with each other forever.

I have never felt so strongly for someone before and, sometimes, I wonder if this whole challenge adds to the excitement of my relationship with Anthony. As they say, 'the more difficult, the more desired, the more appreciated'. I love my long-distance relationship. It gives me plenty of space to continue pursuing my Masters Degree and plenty of time to schedule the most amazing and unforgettable weekends. Since we can't be together all the time, the time that we are together is appreciated so much more. We enjoy every minute and get so much more out of it. I am very much in love with Anthony, completely trust him, and am sure that we will be together as soon as we are both ready.

- Jackie

A long-distance relationship does not have to be as bad as it seems; it all depends on what you make of it.

It is almost three o'clock in the afternoon and today I enjoyed one of the luxuries of a college student with very little work; I sat down and read Loving Your Long-Distance Relationship. Maybe you are curious as to the circumstances of how I got hold of it. I am a sophomore at Tufts University in Medford, Massachusetts, but I am spending this semester in the south of France, in Aix-en-Provence, to be more precise. Apart from trying to improve my French, the main reason for my being here is the fact that my girlfriend, who is a junior at Columbia University in New York City, is spending the semester here as well.

I spent my two weeks of spring vacation back in Boston, where I read a review of your book in our university newspaper. My girlfriend just celebrated her twenty-first birthday yesterday, and I bought your book for her as part of a gift package of twenty-one presents. Obviously, I bought your book for a reason. We have been in a relationship for just over four years, but spent most of it in different places, not necessarily as far away from each other as you and Amanda, but far enough to qualify as a long-distance relationship.

My writing to you has several purposes. Firstly, I wanted to let you know that with every chapter in your book, you precisely reflected what I have been going through for almost three years. It was good to see that there are other people who are experiencing the same thing, and that, in itself, already made me feel less sorry for our situation. Some of the advice you offer is excellent and I know the situations you describe only too well, but I have yet to find a way of dealing with them.

After reading this book, I am confident that I will be able to cope with the problems of a long-distance relationship a little better, and I want to thank you for that. While I was reading your book today, I was telling my girlfriend, who has not read it yet, about some of the situations you describe and the advice you offer. After telling her how much I could relate to you and your situation, the consequence was clear to her: This book has to become my bible for our relationship... and I think it just might.

We first met in high school in Germany and started going out in March of '93, towards the end of my sophomore year and her junior year in high school. Thinking back, I wish I had appreciated more the time I got to spend with her until her graduation, but we did not know any better at the time.

Kerstin graduated in June of '94, and after we spent some time together that summer, she went off to university in London, England, in September. Since we had already been together for a year and a half, there was no question that we were going to stay together because we both felt committed enough to do so. That was how our long-distance relationship started. From September '94 until May '95, she studied in London while I finished my last year of high school in Germany.

We survived those months with many tears, lots of lonely nights, and phone calls. Phone bills in Germany do not list individual calls, just the total cost for all the calls, which made things a bit easier, even though my mother wondered about the sudden increase in the bill. Although I'm sure she knew where the increase stemmed from, she hardly ever made me cut down on the time I spent on the phone with Kerstin, and I will be eternally grateful to her for that. There were lots of letters and I cut down on personal expenses in order to save money for flights -- I even cut down smoking to have more money for plane tickets. Given the fact that London is not that far from Germany, and flights were not that expensive, we got to see each other about once a month for a long weekend, sometimes even a week.

Thinking back to those months, I can completely relate to the 'four-week syndrome' you described in your book and, luckily, we never had to go much longer than that. However, even though we saw each other frequently, I was very troubled with the situation. She knew my life at high school; she had been there and knew all of my friends, while I could not relate to her college life. The fear of her forgetting about her 'little' boyfriend, a year younger, was overwhelming. My insecurity could not be eliminated, even when I went to visit her, meet her new friends, and get a taste of her life. But our commitment to each other was enough to keep her from forgetting about me and to get me over my insecurity.

I had completed applications to universities in the U.S., as well as London, during my senior year and had been accepted to both places. When it was time to make the decision -- most of my friends were going to universities in the Boston area and I am not much of a fan of London -- I decided against going to London, and that led to a very painful breakup between us. Your episode about your last girlfriend and the unwillingness to compromise plans reminded me very much of that situation.

However, after about a week, we decided we loved each other enough to stay together, and in addition to that, she decided to apply for transfer to colleges in the U.S. -- the same schools she was rejected by the year before, which had forced her to attend school in London. In July, she found out that she was accepted to Columbia University in New York City. That day was one of the happiest in our lives, and in early September, she left for New York and I started school in Boston.

The two cities are only about four and a half hours apart, and $49 by Greyhound apart, and although it is very painful at times, I am well aware of the fact that things could be worse. We went through that school year with several downs but always got through them... until we broke up for good in March of '96. I was sick of the long-distance thing, felt like we could not relate to each other's lives anymore, was scared of missing out on other things, and gave in to some of the temptations that college has to offer. The breakup and its aftermath was so ugly that we stopped talking over the summer... until I e-mailed her one day in October, when we were both back at school, more curious to see how she was doing than wanting her back.

After several e-mails, I finally picked up the phone and we talked again. The old feelings started creeping up on me and intensified when I went down to New York a few weeks later. Although we were going to see each other that weekend, I officially went down to visit my brother, who works there, and brought some of our mutual friends down with me as backup.

Although we were both in other relationships with people from our respective schools at the time, we spent an incredible weekend together and did not hold back, either physically or emotionally. After the weekend, we both ended our other relationships and decided to be back together, taking it slowly in order to avoid any possibly painful consequences.

One of the first things Kerstin told me when we got back together in late October, was that she was going to spend the spring semester in France. We both knew that would pose a big threat to our new relationship, because we were not ready to plunge back into a long-distance relationship with an ocean separating us. This time I decided in favor of our relationship immediately, leaving my friends and my familiar college life behind, in order to be with her. It took a lot of organizing -- sophomores are not supposed to go abroad -- but my family and friends were entirely behind me, knowing that this was what I wanted, which was a big help. Reading about the important role your family and friends play in giving advice and support reminded me very much of that situation.

It is late April, and our semester together is coming to an end. During our long-distance times, we always thought that being together for a semester would be paradise... and it is. Every relationship has its problems and some of them do not stem from distance, as I discovered this semester, but it has been an incredible experience, nonetheless. We are not sure about our summer plans yet, but we both know that we will go back to the old New York-to-Boston thing in September. After this semester together and having read your book, I am looking toward it with a positive attitude and am sure that we will get through it. In order to avoid further problems after she graduates in a year, I will most likely work hard enough next school year to finish early and graduate when she does.

Even though we are not sure if we are going to be in the same place after graduation, we are going to try our best to work it out that way... or at least cut the distance to the least possible. But either way, my past experience with Kerstin and your book have taught me that a long-distance relationship does not have to be as bad as it seems; it all depends on what you make of it. And I know that we will get through the last school year, and hopefully, end up with one of the conclusions you propose in your book: to come together permanently. Until then, we will try to stay strong and hope you will do the same. Wishing you all the best.

- Ian

♡♡♡

You can't overemphasize the need for trust in a long-distance relationship. It really is the base ingredient and even though an eye is blind, trust is your best friend. It guides you away from trouble and calms your heart and soul as no words can.

Your book came at a perfect time for me. I've never had long-distance relationships in the past. I decided in June of '97, on my birthday, that I was finished with my boyfriend and the pattern I was in, and borrowed a friend's book, *Soul Mates*, by Thomas Moore. It changed my perspective on love, relationships, and the soul. Anyway, I came home one day and my friend and I were on the phone, and she remarked on the personal ads in the paper and said, "Shel, you gotta hear this thing." She three-way called a dating service in my hometown and I thought it was odd. Odd, but slowly and surprisingly addicting, like Internet chat rooms.

Two days later, I heard this voice. It was magnetic. There was something so different about him. We started sending messages back and forth. A week later I got the courage to call him at his home and we agreed to meet one Saturday at a club we both frequent in Ottawa. (Who knew?) We missed our meeting, essentially because we didn't really know what the other looked like. We agreed to meet the next Saturday. Randy phoned me on the day before our meeting (the second Saturday)

and said, "I have something important to tell you."
I was dying of curiosity. He said, "I can't tell you
now, because I'll only know for sure tomorrow,
and I want to meet you first." The plan was to meet
at the club, get acquainted, then match up on the
dating service with a message to tell each other
what we thought.

I knew when I laid eyes on Randy that this
was potentially "The Guy". We connected on the
system at 3 a.m. and the interest was mutual. So I
asked what the secret was. "Shelley, I signed a
two- year contract to work in Bermuda."

Nevertheless, we dated. I think I would have
felt stupid if I had cut off my contact with him
after that first night. We had six or seven weeks
together. That month and a half was the most
fulfilled, loving time of my entire life. I have never
known a person so like me, and so into me, as I am
into him.

I came across your book when I went to a
mega bookstore in Canada, looking for one of
those little four inch books of creative things to do
on a date. As I flipped through them, I realized I
didn't have enough time to execute half the stuff. I
felt like crying, saw your book, grabbed it, went to

the cash register, then drove home in tears. I
delayed reading your book until after he was gone.
Actually, while he was here, I wanted to keep
putting off The Talk. We talked a little, and I
realized I probably wouldn't have weathered the
first few days of the first week if we hadn't. My
feeling was that I wanted to let go. Randy has said
the same thing, but his concern was that I should
lead an active life, meaning dating others if I
wanted to, because of my age (twenty-two). The
smartest thing I have ever done is to tell him
exactly how I feel, no matter how crazy I felt. If I
hadn't, I would really be hurting.

I wasn't planning on going to the airport with
him but that is what happened. Would I do it
again? Yes and no. It was horrible. Not only my
emotions, but also the look on his face when he
said, "I'll miss you." An 'I don't want to leave you'
look came over his face and he turned and walked
away from me. It has not even been one full
month, but I tell you, the first three days felt like
forever. You totally dread not getting a phone call
during the day, and then the one just before bed,
never really knowing when you will see each other
again. He has asked if I would relocate to

Bermuda. Jobs in my field are supposedly plentiful. I know what you mean about phone bills. It costs $2.50 a minute to call Canada from Bermuda.

But the worst is those agonizing moments when you overanalyse the whole relationship. Even though on Christmas Eve, he called me back at 2 a.m. with a shaky voice and the message, "I called to say, I love you... I really love you," I still think, how do I know? Really know? I can't see his face.

Some of my friends think I need a good shrink, but I swear I may end up with this man the rest of my life. It really feels like a day-by-day experience, nothing for sure, at least not unless he moves or I move. When you write your next book, make sure to emphasize that you must really talk before the person leaves. It caused me a lot of tears until I found out my fears were unfounded.

- Shelley

People say we're on holiday, because we've never faced the day-to-day stresses. I'll grant them that. However, we face many stresses that everyday sort-of couples don't have to contend with, the trust issue being a big one.

♡♡♡

I just felt compelled to share my story with you after reading your website. I was divorced a year and a half ago, and have custody of my two-year-old son, so a social life wasn't exactly easy. I would talk to people on the net as a form of socialization, but never expected anything to come of it.

I met Mikael by fluke, when his computer crashed and he accidentally ended up with my name on his contact list. When I found out he was from Stockholm, Sweden (I'm from Toronto), I figured I'd just have someone interesting to talk to. As the months passed, things began to feel like more than friendship; we shared all our thoughts and past experiences with ex-spouses, etc. Phone calls began, and slowly we felt our relationship begin to change from friendship to romance. We weren't sure if it would be different once we met, but we knew we had to find out.

After months of waiting (distance was already difficult and expensive, due to phone bills!), Mikael came to Toronto to spend the Christmas holidays. It was love, the best two weeks of our lives. The enjoyment was brought down by the reality of him having to go back to Sweden. He's back there now, and I'm learning the hard way just how stressful a long-distance relationship can be. It takes a lot of trust, less sleep because of the six hour time difference, and a lot of perseverance. Until he can go through the legalities of moving to Canada, we have to rely on short phone calls, e-mail, and the Internet.

So far, we've been able to spread things out so that we can meet every seven or eight weeks. I'm going there for a week, then we're meeting in New York for a few days, and then it's his turn to come here again. (This can really drain the wallet!) We are adamant about making this work. So many skeptics are out there, and we're hellbent on proving them wrong. People say we're on holiday, because we've never faced the day-to-day stresses. I'll grant them that. However, we face many stresses that everyday sort-of couples don't have to contend with, the trust issue being a big one.

I thank you for the website and I'm going out tomorrow to find Loving Your Long-Distance Relationship. Now I'll have something to read on the long plane ride over there, and something to leave for him when I have to go back.

- Karen

To anyone who is committed to a long-distance relationship, do not give up hope. If it's any comfort, know that people like you everywhere are going through the same thing and loving/hating every moment of it.
- Stephen Blake

A hug, a kiss, a moment with your face in view. Your lingering scent, the warmth of your touch... so reminiscent of the miracle of you.

♡♡♡

I didn't want to fall in love. At least not with him. He wasn't my type. You know, the tall, overconfident ones who smile just the right way, catching a girl off guard! No, I certainly didn't want to fall in love. Not then. We didn't have anything in common. I kept telling him *that* every time we met. Besides, he was leaving for England soon, so it couldn't work. At least not until that Saturday. We shouldn't have sat in that cozy corner of the Chateau Laurier Hotel, watching those wedding parties scamper by. We shouldn't have laughed quite so much over our ideas for a crazy movie we'd like to write. He shouldn't have told me I was the angel girl in a misty dream he'd had years ago. Why did he have to make me fall in love with him one week before he left?

Driving home today, I was wishing I could have spent more time with him. Although his written words are better than no contact at all, he is a much more dynamic character in person. Of course, I'm in no way commenting on his writing style. But I've lost some of that character without being able to talk to him face-to-face: that smile of his, those kind, sometimes sad eyes, his laugh, even the way he held my hand. I'm missing those things.

There is a creative, individualistic spirit within him. I kept my guard up until I realized we carry a similar spirit: a bit lonely, sometimes melancholy, distinctly unique, finding joy in higher revelations. To date, I've found this in no man save him. That Saturday, it was as if my spirit dared to defy my rational mind, peeked out of its shell, saw his spirit, and was captivated from that moment on.

The words, "I miss you", have become a cliche in our letters. It's the most obvious phrase to complete our phone conversations. We say it every time. Cliche, yes. Meaningless, no. For in those three words, we convey the knowledge of the deep consciousness within us that is now well-acquainted with the dearth of the other. May it remain poignant until we meet again.

A hug, a kiss, a moment with your face in view. Your lingering scent, the warmth of your touch... so reminiscent of the miracle of you.

- Shauna

Trust must have time to grow and solidify before a relationship can take a cross-country move. Make sure you know your partner well before getting into an LDR.

I have been in a long-distance relationship for a year and a half now. I met my boyfriend at work. I knew him a year before we starting dating, and then a month later, he went away to college. We e-mailed every day, called each other once a week, and visited each other about every two months. That point in our relationship was difficult, considering we hardly knew each other and we were both new to this.

When he came back for the summer, I was so happy that we were finally going to spend some time together, but little did I know that this would only be the beginning of an even greater task. Moises, my boyfriend, didn't do so well in his freshmen year in college, so he had to move even farther away to live with his brother in Atlanta. I was upset and we fought about it, but he insisted that this was the only way. He couldn't stay in Pennsylvania because none of his family was living here, and I couldn't go with him since my college is here. We never really resolved the issue of his leaving, but he still left. He told me that if the relationship ever ends, he would know it was his fault for leaving me here by myself. He said, "What kind of man would leave his woman in another state?" Obviously him!

I'm still not happy with the situation and I don't think I ever will be. He now loves it in Atlanta and doesn't think he'll ever leave. He's building a life for himself down there and expects me to move when I finish school in two years. I know it would be a great opportunity for me to start off my career, but I don't know if I could ever leave my life as I know it. I have my friends and my family here. I love Moises greatly and I want things to work out, but I don't know how to do that anymore. Every time I see him, it's as if I don't know him. We do great while talking on the phone, but we don't know how to bring our worlds together. I know he loves me and I know he's planning on marrying me as soon as I finish school.

If someone were to ask me if they should get involved in an LDR, I would tell them not to. It's painful, and depressing! A person needs to feel loved and have the attention they need, every day. I have thought of giving up my life in Pennsylvania and running away to Atlanta, but would that be what I really want? I'd be giving up my college and the career I've always dreamed of. My family and friends would become my new LDRs. I've had wonderful times with Moises, but the distance is hurting our relationship. I don't know how to cope with it anymore. I also wonder if I'm wasting my time on the wrong person. If he really loved me, don't you think he would find a way for us to be together, especially since he's the one who put us in this predicament? I could handle him being away at college and seeing him during breaks and the summer, but not this. I hope our story has a happy ending, and maybe we'll both come to terms and figure something out that we can agree on. I'll read your book and see if I can find something to help me survive the next two years.

- Jennifer

True love has no time line but is, rather, a unique experience that makes life worth living.

It's almost 3 a.m.... and I am dreading this day. For a couple of months now, I have thought about what life will be like without my beloved Sarah. Sure, I'm only nineteen and my love life is still young, but it feels like I have spent the best days of my life with her. These days have been filled with all of the emotions and experiences that everyone wishes for, at least once in a lifetime, and I thank God for them.

Today Sarah is leaving for Switzerland on a four-month exchange. I know that this is a relatively short amount of time for some people, but any long separation from her creates a void in my life. I have never experienced anything like this before. I now know this is true love, and I can't wait for our future together, when she comes home in June. Having her come home will be better than winning the lottery.

Sarah will always hold a special place in my heart, and the flame of our love will never burn out.

True love tests all of the emotions. True love has no time line but is, rather, a unique experience that makes life worth living. I will miss her greatly, and I love her with all of my heart.

- John

♡♡♡

Take a little box and put a compass in it, with little heart confetti, and a very small note in it that says, "You can always use this to find your way home to my heart."

♡♡♡

I have a neat story that I thought I'd tell you. It illustrates how a long-distance relationship can really work great, and in the end, lead to a lifetime of happiness. The story is about my parents and how they met.

My mother lived in Ohio and she has an older brother who enlisted in the army, way back in the late '60s. His name is David. Well, David met my father at the army base and they became really close buddies. My dad is from Pennsylvania and got along with my Uncle David really well. One day, my uncle said, "Hey, how about you come home and meet my family? I have a sister... she might like you."

So Dad went home with David and met my mother. The funniest thing about this story is that my mom thought my dad was gross when she first met him and, in fact, her mother didn't like him either... but my dad fell in love with my mom at first sight.

After the visit, my dad went back to the base, but he couldn't get my mom off his mind. He sent her letters and cards... and then he started driving from Pennsylvania to Ohio for the weekends. Eight hours on the road to get there and eight hours more to get back. He loved her a lot... and after awhile, I guess my mom just sorta fell in love with the big lug. He sent her roses and packages, candies, cards, romantic love letters... and finally, after all that, they decided to get married.

They stayed together the whole time he was in the service, and like clockwork, my dad would go and visit her every weekend. I love to see the pictures that my dad sent to my mom, him posing near tanks and stuff... it's a riot! And then there are the pictures of my mom with her 'Barry' shirt on. It's so neat. And today, they still love each other so much... they've been together for 20 some years now.

I think they are the greatest... and I think their story is the neatest. And what's funny is, I think the

LDR thing has been passed down to me, because I'm in love with a Georgia boy. We hardly ever get to see each other.... but it's like he's my soul mate. We send each other all sorts of little things just to make it more interesting and to keep the flow going. I think that's a good key for a successful LDR. Sending little... well, I call them care packages... things that remind the other of the person they're missing, like a guy's favourite shirt sprayed with his cologne, or a little teddy bear with the girl's perfume on it... sweet love letters, things like that. I think the coolest idea is one I gave my best friend, Traci, for her army boy, Matt. Take a little box and put a compass in it, with little heart confetti, and a very small note in it that says, "You can always use this to find your way home to my heart."

- Jessica

True love tests all of the emotions.

We trust one another, we communicate well, and most of all, we have the basis for any good relationship: we are the best of friends.

♡♡♡

It all began in the summer of '94. I was a student starting her first semester at Orange Coast College and never expected that I would meet my soul mate that semester. It was the typical meeting: a college party. My friend, Fredrik, invited me to go with him. It was enjoyable; lots of new faces and interesting personalities.

It was there I met him. Michael. It was not the storybook romance beginning. Neither love at first sight nor even lust at first sight. I was actually not very impressed with him! He was being very flirtatious with my friend, Mary Ann, and a little towards me as well. I thought he was your typical Casanova! I was actually attracted to his roommate, Henrik.

Later on campus, I ran into Henrik and we traded phone numbers. The next weekend, I decided to call him up and guess who answered the phone? Yes, Michael! To my amazement, he was totally down to earth and easy to talk to. We ended up talking on the phone for an hour and I almost forgot the reason for my phone call: to speak with Henrik! From that point on, it was instant friendship. Within the first year, I felt like I'd known him all my life. He was my confidant, my pep-talker, my study buddy, and my best friend.

You're probably wondering where the long-distance comes in. Well, Michael was an exchange student from Sweden, and after his first year of school in California, he went home to Sweden for two months during the summer. It was a difficult time for me, because I was so used to seeing him almost every day, but during that time we kept in touch via fax and telephone.

Three months after he returned, we became a couple. We had an overwhelming love affair which lasted a year and then ended for several reasons. Basically, it was the wrong timing for us. We loved each other, but love wasn't enough to keep us together, because we both needed to mature on our own. After Michael received his degree, he returned to his home country. I was fortunate to have the chance to see his country. Despite all the difficult times and fights we went through, we remained the best of friends. We spent a wonderful month together travelling the Scandinavian countries and appreciating the time we had left together. Leaving Michael was the most heart-wrenching thing I ever had to do, but I had to go back to California.

The first month back home was awful. Every single place brought back memories I shared with him. But I knew I had to get back on my feet and empower myself. Slowly but surely, my wounds healed and I got my life back on track. During this growth period, we remained in touch via phone. It still hurt to talk to him, but our best friendship kept our bond intact. We both grew up a lot living our own separate lives, but our love still remained.

Is there a happy ending to this story? Yes. The old cliche, "absence makes the heart grow fonder," applies to our relationship. The distance apart actually strengthened our relationship as well as our love for one another. We are now officially back together again. Of course, it's very difficult to be away from the one you love, but we stay in touch frequently via phone, e-mail, and care packages.

We trust one another, we communicate well, and most of all, we have the basis for any good relationship: we are the best of friends. We both know the distance is only temporary. Either of us can relocate. But it is my goal to move to Europe with him. My chosen career can take me anywhere in the world, and as we speak, I'm working on living with Michael permanently, in Europe, within a year and a half.

Long-distance relationships can work if there's love, trust, understanding, and faith. It's working out for Michael and me, and we're both confident that it will continue until we are living together in the same country.

- Nora

His simple touch, even if for just a few days every three months, is enough to make it all worth it.

My boyfriend, Nathan, and I have been together since our freshman year. The summer before senior year, he moved to Naples, Florida from Byron, Illinois. We used to be inseparable, but now we only get to see each other every three months or so. I love him so much, and it is very hard to wonder when the next visit with each other will be. Everyone thinks we are crazy, and they all wonder how we can handle being so far apart. I trust Nathan and he trusts me. I have a lot of pride knowing that I'm a teenager in a successful long-distance relationship.

When we do get to see each other... it is wonderful. We spend most of our time just talking. It's amazing what we took for granted before he left. Just holding his hand while shopping makes me smile with happiness. His simple touch, even if for just a few days every three months, is enough to make it all worth it. I don't know what will come of this relationship, since college is coming. Neither of us can afford the out-of-state tuition for Florida or Illinois, but we're trying to think of other solutions. I'm looking into a private school down in Florida and maybe that will pan out, but only time will tell. My best advice for keeping a long-distance relationship is trust. We don't e-mail everyday or call, but that is because we don't have to. I know that when we aren't writing or calling, we are thinking about each other. I think Nathan would say the same thing.

- Kendra

I believe with all my heart that if we make it through this, we will be able to conquer anything. Nothing will be able to stop our love.

I was the U.S. Marine photojournalist who wrote a few days ago. I was surprised to see an e-mail asking for the rest of my story. I'll start with the present. Currently I'm sitting onboard an amphibious ship off the coast of Thessoloniki, Greece. There are more than 2,400 people onboard but sometimes I feel like I'm the only one. I'm not weird and I don't have any mental disabilities. I'm just in love with the girl of my dreams and missing her very much. Now to the beginning..

I was working about 40 hours a week at a family restaurant in eastern North Carolina in December 1996, and at the same time, answering my call to serve my country. It had been more than 30 days since my last day off of work. I was getting burned out and needed a day off, but the restaurant couldn't afford to let me go because the wait staff was so short-handed. The manager informs me a couple of days later that she had hired two new girls, and that after I trained them to standards, then I could have three days off. I was ecstatic.

I inquired about the new employees. She told me that they were both named Jennifer and one was an extremely attractive blonde. I laughed and said, "Me and blondes don't mix and I've had a bad history with girls named Jenny." The next day, running late as usual, I wheeled into the parking lot, turned off my car, grabbed my tie, and hustled for the door. I was tying my tie, when I turned the corner and BAM! There she stood. She was the most beautiful woman I had ever laid eyes on.

Now I was never a shy guy with women, but I wasn't very confident either. But the very moment our eyes met, I just knew she would be mine. I had never believed in love at first sight until that moment. She stole my heart when she said, "Hello, I'm Jenny. You must be Jon." So we talked and laughed and I taught her how to wait tables at this restaurant. We got to know each other quite well within a few short days.

She was dating someone, but within days, I had plucked her precious heart from his hands. On my first day off, I went and made a personalized card and bought some candles. I put it all in a bag along with a poem I wrote just for her. I didn't tell her who it was from but she knew. I wrote on the note, "One night we will drink wine by the candle light from these candles."

We quickly fell in love and knew that our love was based on truth, faith, honesty, and the things that make love pure, and not the distractions that sex bring into a developing relationship.

We had a deep, romantic fall in love. We went sailing, roller-skating, took walks on the beach, enjoyed nice dinners, and long talks. Several months later, I took her home with me and my family immediately gave the head-nodding sign of approval. (She is just as beautiful and pure on the inside as she is on the outside.)

I've had to leave her several times seeing that I am a U.S. Marine and all. But this six-month deployment to the Mediterrean Sea is testing our love. I told her on the first date that I don't play head games, I wouldn't give her any heartaches or headaches, and that I could show her a wonderful place called love. The funny thing is that she has taken me to a place I've never seen and it is more beautiful, pure, sacred, and true than I ever thought imaginable. The name of that place is true love.

I believe with all my heart that if we make it through this, we will be able to conquer anything. Nothing will be able to stop our love. I send her at least an e-mail a day, and I usually either write her a letter, work on a video tape or an audio tape (love songs included). About once a week I call her, and I call her every day while we are in port.

I have nothing to hide, no reason to lie or fabricate material, and no motives other than sharing with the world that wonderful blessing from above, called true love.

- Jon

Conclusion

And you know, that as hard as it was, you'd go through it all again, and then again, if it would get you here, standing in front of your family and friends, promising to love each other... forever.
- Kimberli Bryan

P reparing these letters for publication has been a touching experience for me. It's brought back a flood of memories from the time when my husband, Gary, and I were living in different states, wildly in love, and wanting nothing more than to be together every moment. As I began to write this, I realized that everything I wanted to say I had said before, when I wrote our marriage vows. No one who heard these words the day we were married understood what they truly meant as well as you will if you're missing your love. They represented for us the end of a painful journey. My wish is that they give you hope on yours.

Love, true love, is a force of nature, unequalled. It's both wonderful and terrible, the best and worst thing that can happen to any of us. And happen is exactly what it does… like hurricanes happen. There you are, happily living your well-planned life, with your future neatly mapped out and everything moving along just as you think it should. Then, on a perfectly ordinary day, you meet someone and your heart stops beating, and suddenly everything you thought you wanted out of life is meaningless unless that person is with you.

Your life has changed forever. No matter how happy you thought you were, you can never go back to the way things were before your heart stopped, before you knew it was possible to feel so much for someone. And that's when it can be terrible. Sometimes there are compelling reasons to walk away from that person. Sometimes circumstances dictate that walking away is the only sane thing to do. And you might try to do that. You might try a thousand times and still fail, because it's a lot like deciding not to breathe anymore. And if you do manage to walk away, you soon realize that you're just a hollow shell of the person you were, because living without your heart isn't much like living.

So you just move heaven and earth to be together with the person who holds your heart. There's no limit to the amount of emotional pain that two people in love can endure in the hope that someday they'll be together.

You survive the terrible by living and reliving, a thousand times over in your mind, the incomparable wonder of the moments you spend together. When that person walks into the room and angels sing and stars fall and your heart stops beating, again… every time. When one hug can make up for a hundred hours of loneliness, and a smile makes you cry because it's so beautiful. You know that no matter how bad it gets, as soon as you're together again, a single kiss will make the world a wonderful place to be.

And you know, that as hard as it was, you'd

go through it all again, and then again, if it would get you here, standing in front of your family and friends, promising to love each other... forever.

- Kimberli Bryan, author of *Loving Your Long-Distance Relationship for Women.*

P.S. You can e-mail me or Stephen Blake directly through Anton Publishing's website at www.sblake.com, or write to us at the following address:

Anton Publishing Inc.
305 Madison Ave.
Suite 1166
New York, New York 10165.

Order *Loving Your Long-Distance Relationship*, *Still Loving*, or *Loving Your Long-Distance Relationship for Women.*

To order, send this page along with a check or money order for $6.99 U.S. or $9.99 Canadian each plus $2. shipping and handling for one copy, 50¢ shipping and handling for each additional copy, to:

Anton Publishing
305 Madison Ave
Suite 1166
New York, New York 10165

Book Title(s) _____

Name _____

Address _____

City _____ State/Province _____

Zip/Postal Code _____